...e gray with
dark forehead

...ean
...rbler

white chin, thin
breast band,
female
duller

Indigo Bunting

blue with
dark wings

female brown

male

Tree Swallow

white chin
and chest

Eastern Bluebird

sky blue with
rusty chest,
female duller

Barn Swallow

orange forehead,
forked tail,
female duller

Blue Grosbeak

rusty wing bars

female brown

male

female

Purple Martin

nearly black,
notched tail,
female gray
belly

male

4"   4"   5 1/2"   5 1/2"   7"   7"   7"   8 1/2"

Florida Scrub-Jay
blue with white forehead

Blue Jay
blue crest, black necklace

Belted Kingfisher
shaggy crest, female has two bands on chest

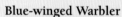

Mostly yellow

Blue-winged Warbler
yellow cap, black eye line, dark eyes, female duller

Tennessee Warbler
grayish chin and chest, female less gray

Wilson's Warbler
black cap, female lacks cap

female

American Goldfinch

male

black forehead, female lacks black forehead

11" 12" 13" 4 1/2" 4 3/4" 4 3/4" 5"

Mostly yellow

American Redstart

yellow patches, white belly

male orange

female

Common Yellowthroat

black mask, female lacks mask

Magnolia Warbler

black necklace, thick streaks on chest, female less black

Orange-crowned Warbler

dull yellow, thin bill

Prairie Warbler

chestnut streaks on back

Worm-eating Warbler

black line through dark eyes, striped head

Yellow Warbler

orange streaks on chest, female lacks streaks

Kentucky Warbler

black cap, yellow around eyes

5"   5"   5"   5"   5"   5"   5"   5"

Mostly yellow

Hooded Warbler

black chin and head patch, female partial patch

Palm Warbler

chestnut cap, yellow eyebrows

Pine Warbler

yellow eye-ring, white wing bars, female duller

Prothonotary Warbler

yellow with gray wings

female

Dickcissel

black bib, female lacks bib

male

Scarlet Tanager

yellowish with dark wings

male red

female

Yellow-breasted Chat

yellow chin and chest, white around eyes

Baltimore Oriole

pale yellow, white wing bars

male orange

female

5 1/4" 5 1/2" 5 1/2" 5 1/2" 6" 7" 7 1/2" 7 1/2"

Mostly yellow

Orchard Oriole

dull yellow, white wing bars

male orange

female

Summer Tanager

large bill

male red

female

Evening Grosbeak

female

bright yellow eyebrows, large ivory bill, female duller

male

Eastern Meadowlark

black V on chest, white outer tail feathers as seen in flight

Mostly orange

American Redstart

orange patches

female yellow

male

Orchard Oriole

black head, rusty body

female yellow

male

Baltimore Oriole

black head, white wing bars

female yellow

male

7 1/2"   8"   8"   9"   5"   7 1/2"   7 1/2"

House Finch

brown cap

female brown

male

Purple Finch

red cap

female brown

male

Scarlet Tanager

black wings
and tail

female yellow

male

Summer Tanager

overall red

female yellow

male

Northern Cardinal

black mask,
red crest, red bill

male

female brown

5" 6" 7" 8" 8 1/2"

Brown Creeper
long curved bill

House Finch
brown cap, streaked flanks and belly

male red

female

Pine Siskin
yellow streaks on wings, female less yellow

Chipping Sparrow
rusty cap, clear chest

Chimney Swift
pointed head and tail as seen in flight

Chestnut-sided Warbler

yellow cap, chestnut sides, female duller

House Wren
short curved bill

Carolina Wren
white eyebrows, white markings on sides of neck

5" 5" 5" 5" 5" 5" 5" 5 1/2"

Dark-eyed Junco
brown with white belly

male gray

Song Sparrow
central dark spot on streaked chest

female

Cliff Swallow
tan-to-rust forehead and cheeks

Northern Rough-winged Swallow
plain brown with gray belly

Indigo Bunting
brown with lighter throat

male blue

Purple Finch
white eye stripe

male red

female

female

Hermit Thrush
dark spots on chest, rusty tail

Louisiana Waterthrush
heavily streaked chest, white eyebrows

5 1/2"   5 1/2"   5 1/2"   5 1/2"   5 1/2"   6"   6"   6"

Mostly brown

American Tree Sparrow

rusty cap, central dark spot on clear chest

female

House Sparrow

black throat, gray cap, female tan eyebrows

male

Lark Sparrow

bold head pattern, central dark spot on white chest

White-throated Sparrow

white chin, bold eyebrows

White-crowned Sparrow

black and white head

Fox Sparrow

heavily streaked chest and belly

Blue Grosbeak

brown with tan wing bars

male blue

female

Rose-breasted Grosbeak

bold white eyebrows

female

male black & white

6"   6"   6 1/2"   6 1/2"   7"   7"   7"   7 1/2"

Brown-headed Cowbird

whitish throat

male black

female

Horned Lark

white-to-yellow throat, black necklace, female duller

Eastern Towhee

rusty sides, red eyes

male black

female

Cedar Waxwing

black mask, red wing tips

Wood Thrush

rusty head, black spots on chest and belly

Bohemian Waxwing

black mask, white and red wing tips

Red-winged Blackbird

light eyebrows

male black

female

Northern Cardinal

black mask, red bill

male red

female

7 1/2"   7 1/2"   7 1/2"   7 1/2"   8"   8 1/4"   8 1/2"   8 1/2"

Common Nighthawk

white chin, white band across wings as seen in flight, female tan chin

Whip-poor-will

large dark eyes, gray on back

Northern Bobwhite

white eyebrows and chin, female tan eyebrows and chin

Killdeer

two black bands around neck

Brown Thrasher

long tail, long curved bill

Chuck-will's-widow

big head, large dark eyes, small bill

Yellow-billed Cuckoo

white chin, dark bars on long tail

Mourning Dove

blue eye-ring, bobs head while walking

9"   10"   10"   11"   11"   12"   12"   12"

Mostly brown

Northern Flicker

yellow wing linings, black mark on face, female lacks black mark

Boat-tailed Grackle

brown head, long tail, dark eyes

male black

female

Ruffed Grouse

dark ruffs

female

Wild Turkey

bare skin on head, black beard, female lacks beard

male

Mostly gray

Golden-crowned Kinglet

gold and orange on head, female lacks orange

Ruby-crowned Kinglet

white wing bars

Northern Parula

gray head, yellow throat and chest

Brown-headed Nuthatch

brown cap, white cheeks

12"   15"   17 1/2"   42"   4"   4"   4"   4 1/2"

Mostly gray

Red-breasted Nuthatch

black eye line, female gray cap

White-eyed Vireo

yellow on flanks and face, white eyes

Black-capped Chickadee

black cap, white cheeks, white wing edges

Carolina Chickadee

black cap, gray cheeks, gray wing edges

Dark-eyed Junco

white belly, pink bill

female brown

male

White-breasted Nuthatch

black cap, white cheeks, female duller cap

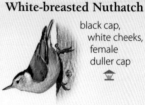

Yellow-rumped Warbler

white chin, bold yellow patches, female duller

Yellow-throated Warbler

yellow chin, black face, female duller

4 1/2"   5"   5"   5"   5 1/2"   5 1/2"   5 1/2"   5 1/2"

Warbling Vireo

small bill, white eyebrows, dark eyes

Red-eyed Vireo

white eye line, red eyes

Tufted Titmouse

large crest

Common Ground-Dove

gray nape, dark-tipped red bill

Eastern Phoebe

pumps tail up and down while perched

Great Crested Flycatcher

yellow belly, long rusty tail

Eastern Kingbird

white-tipped tail

Gray Catbird

chestnut patch under tail

5 1/2"   6"   6"   6 1/2"   7"   8"   8"   9"

Loggerhead Shrike
black mask

Northern Mockingbird
long tail, white wing bars

American Robin
black head, female gray head

White-winged Dove
blue ring around eyes, white wing edges

Eurasian Collared-Dove
thin black line on neck

Rock Pigeon
variety of colors

Mostly black & white

Black-and-white Warbler
black throat and cheeks, female lacks black patches

Downy Woodpecker
short bill, red spot, female lacks red spot

9"   10"   10"   11"   12 1/2"   13"   5"   6"

Red-cockaded Woodpecker

black cap, white face

Rose-breasted Grosbeak

rose chest patch

female brown

male

Yellow-bellied Sapsucker

red cap and chin, female white chin and throat

Hairy Woodpecker

large bill, red spot, female lacks red spot

Red-headed Woodpecker

red head

Red-bellied Woodpecker

red cap and nape, female gray cap

Pileated Woodpecker

red crest and mustache, female black forehead

7"   7 1/2"   8 1/2"   9"   9"   9 1/4"   19"

Mostly black

Brown-headed Cowbird

brown head, gray bill

male

female brown

European Starling

bill yellow in summer, gray in winter

Eastern Towhee

black head and chest, red eyes

female brown

male

Red-winged Blackbird

red and yellow shoulder patches

female brown

male

Common Grackle

blue head, long tail, female shorter tail

Boat-tailed Grackle

very long tail, yellow eyes

female brown

male

Fish Crow

black with nasal "cah" call

American Crow

black with familiar "caw" call

7 1/2" 7 1/2" 7 1/2" 8 1/2" 12" 15" 16" 18"

Mostly black

Common Raven

shaggy throat feathers

Mostly green

Ruby-throated Hummingbird

ruby throat, female lacks ruby throat

Painted Bunting

female

blue head, orange chest, female all green

male

Monk Parakeet

gray forehead, chin and chest

24 1/2"   3 1/4"   5 1/2"   12"